Zoom In on Rain Forest Animals

Jaguars

Leo Statts

abdopublishing.com

Published by Abdo Zoom™, PO Box 398166, Minneapolis, Minnesota 55439. Copyright © 2017 by Abdo Consulting Group, Inc. International copyrights reserved in all countries. No part of this book may be reproduced in any form without written permission from the publisher. Abdo Zoom™ is a trademark and logo of Abdo Consulting Group, Inc.

Printed in the United States of America, North Mankato, Minnesota
062016
092016

THIS BOOK CONTAINS RECYCLED MATERIALS

Cover Photo: Shutterstock Images
Interior Photos: Anan Kaewkhammul/Shutterstock Images, 1; Matt Gibson/iStockphoto, 4; Sarah Cheriton-Jones/iStockphoto, 5; Stef Bennett/iStockphoto, 7; iStockphoto, 8, 10–11, 14; Shutterstock Images, 9, 16; Red Line Editorial, 11, 20 (left), 20 (right), 21 (left), 21 (right); Dicky Singh/iStockphoto, 12; Matthew Hart/iStockphoto, 13; Kevin Autret/Shutterstock Images, 16–17; Michael Fitzsimmons/iStockphoto, 18, 19

Editor: Brienna Rossiter
Series Designer: Madeline Berger
Art Direction: Dorothy Toth

Publisher's Cataloging-in-Publication Data
Names: Statts, Leo, author.
Title: Jaguars / by Leo Statts.
Description: Minneapolis, MN : Abdo Zoom, [2017] | Series: Rain forest animals | Includes bibliographical references and index.
Identifiers: LCCN 2016941142 | ISBN 9781680791945 (lib. bdg.) | ISBN 9781680793628 (ebook) | ISBN 9781680794519 (Read-to-me ebook)
Subjects: LCSH: Jaguars--Juvenile literature.
Classification: DDC 599.75--dc23
LC record available at http://lccn.loc.gov/2016941142

Table of Contents

Jaguars 4

Body 8

Habitat 10

Food 14

Life Cycle 18

Quick Stats. 20

Glossary 22

Booklinks 23

Index 24

Jaguars

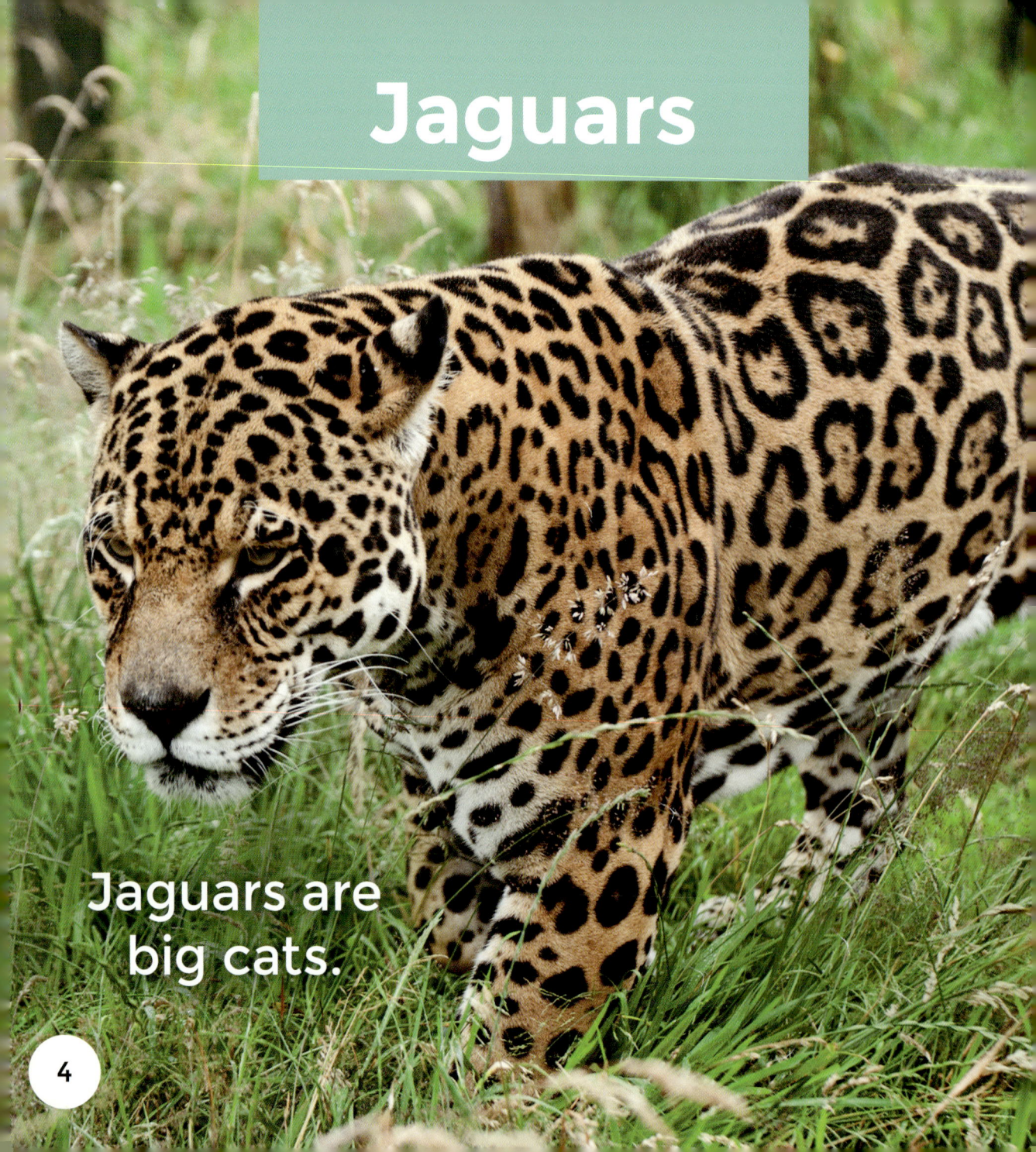

Jaguars are big cats.

They have tan or orange fur.
It has black spots called **rosettes**.

Some jaguars are completely black. Their spots are hard to see.

Body

A jaguar has a long tail.
It has sharp teeth.

Its bite is twice as strong as a lion's bite.

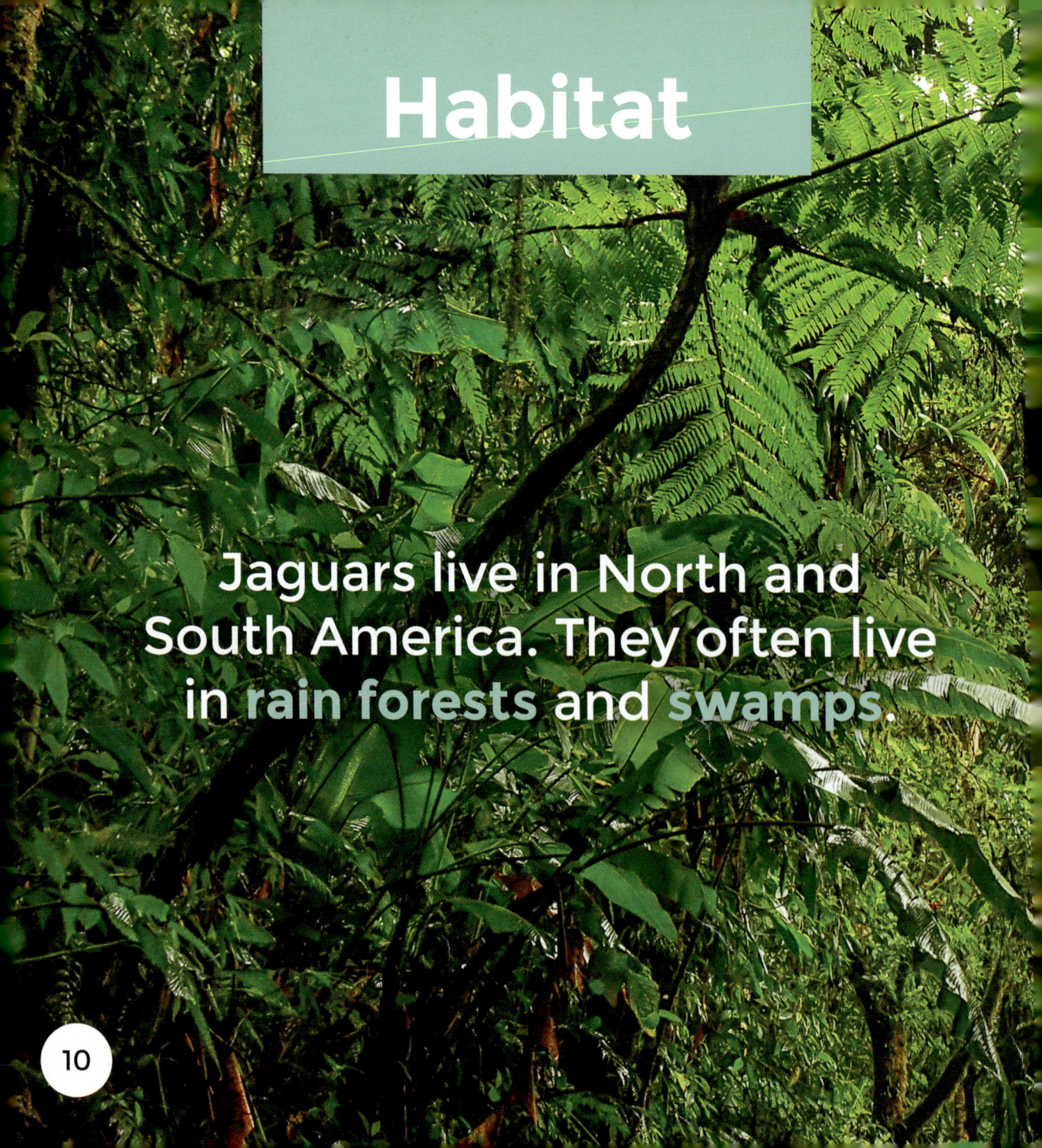

Habitat

Jaguars live in North and South America. They often live in **rain forests** and **swamps**.

☐ Where jaguars live

Jaguars live in areas with lots of plants.

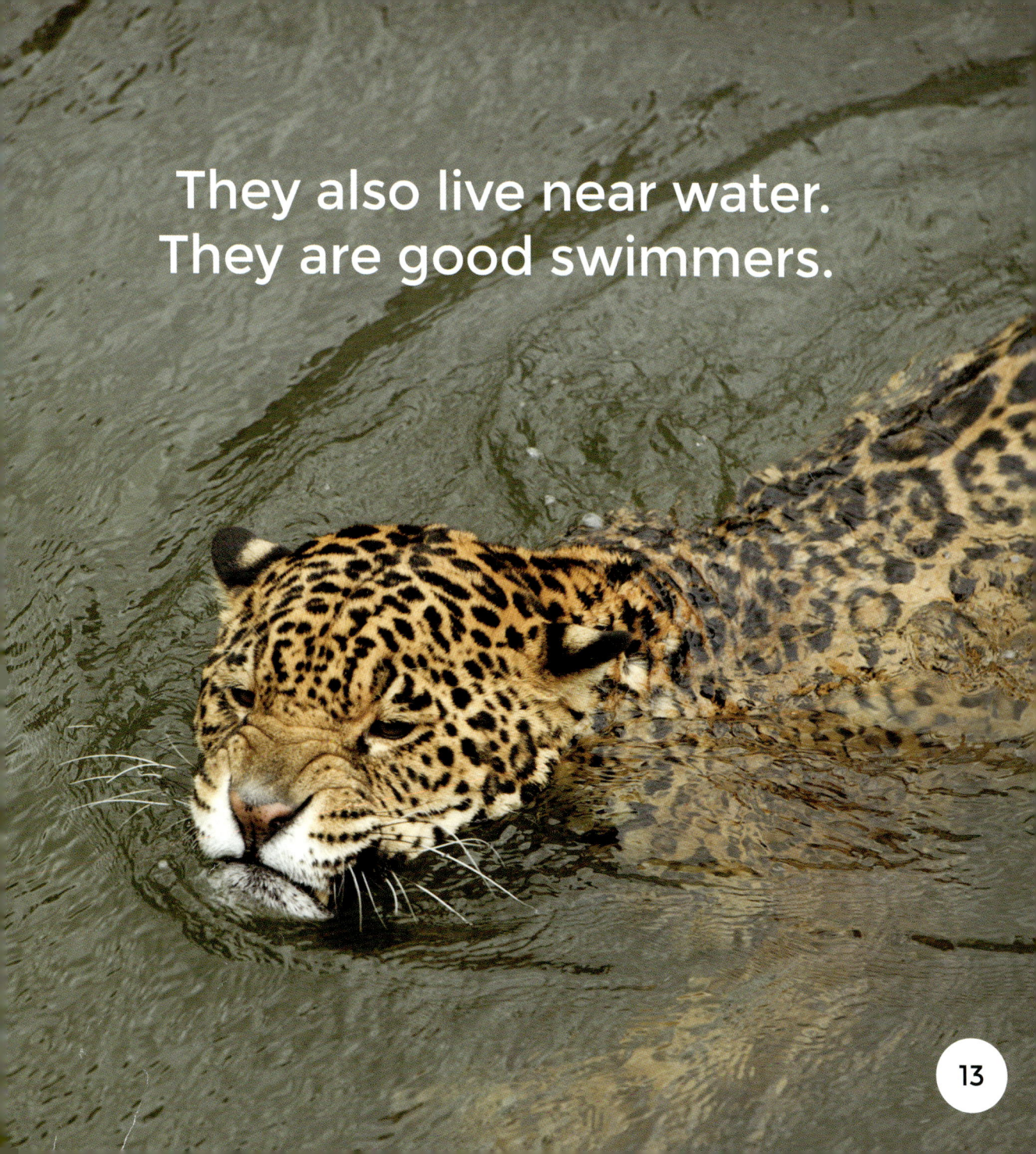
They also live near water.
They are good swimmers.

Food

Jaguars eat meat. They eat deer, fish, and turtles. They can bite through a turtle's shell.

Jaguars usually hunt on the ground. Sometimes they hide in trees.

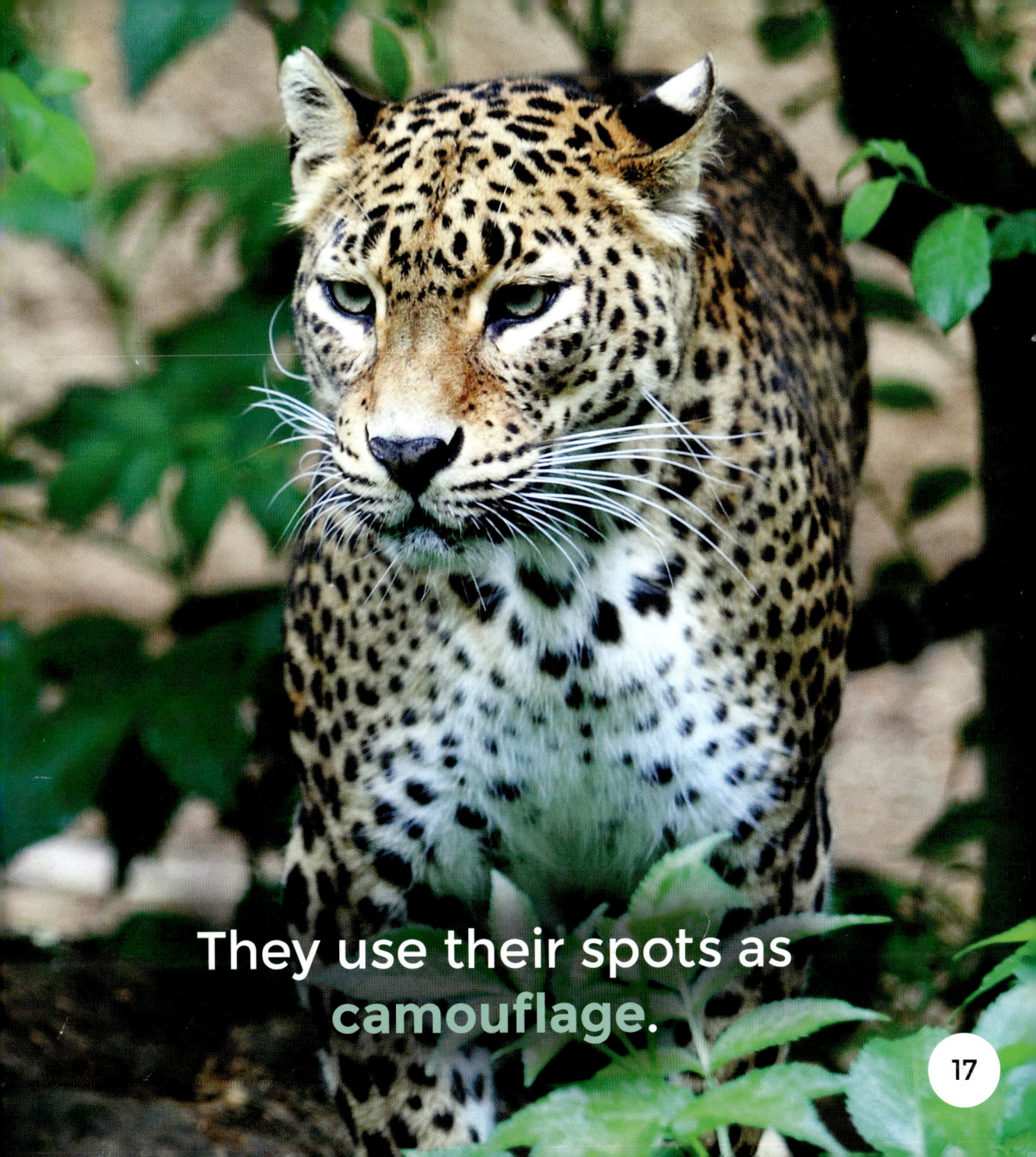

They use their spots as **camouflage.**

Life Cycle

Jaguars have one to four cubs at a time. They can live 15 years in the wild.

Average Length

A jaguar is longer than a sofa.

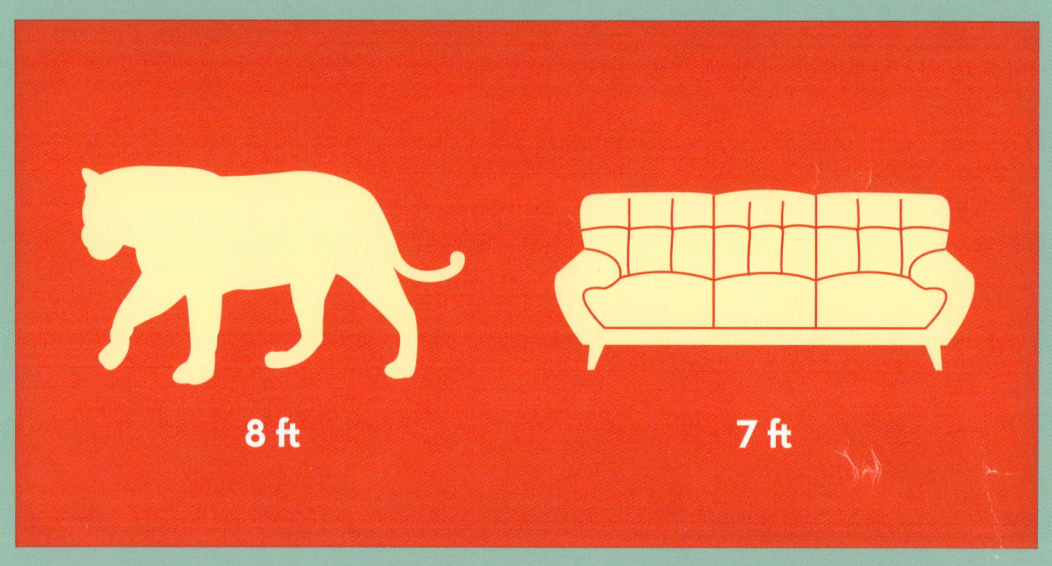

8 ft   7 ft

Average Weight

A jaguar is nearly as heavy as a refrigerator.

Glossary

camouflage - something that helps an animal hide by making it look like its surroundings.

cub - a young animal.

rain forest - a tropical woodland where it rains a lot.

rosette - a marking that looks like a rose.

swamp - wet land that is filled with trees, plants, or both.

Booklinks

For more information on **jaguars**, please visit booklinks.abdopublishing.com

Zoom In on Animals!

Learn even more with the Abdo Zoom Animals database. Check out **abdozoom.com** for more information.

Index

black, 5, 6

cubs, 19

fur, 5

hunt, 16

meat, 15

rain forests, 10

South America, 10

spots, 5, 6, 17

swamps, 10

tail, 8

teeth, 8